C++

CODING CHEATSHEET

{GOAT edition}

Not just another C++ book.

Because there is enough theoretical knowledge.

We give you the real code design and engineering optimization knowledge you lack which is attained only after a decade of real coding experience.

Edition v1.0

Wesley Kincaid 🖐

1

INTRODUCTION

This book will change your C++ programming skills forever. Read it now to level up your future.

This book **"C++: Coding Cheatsheet: GOAT edition** " is the only book you need to master C++ programming concepts. The focus is on practical programming skills, design concepts and performance engineering ideas.

This book include:

- Chapters covering all core concepts in C++ programming, code design and optimization including:
  - OOP concepts, Inheritance, Composition, Singleton pattern
  - Efficient use of C++ STL for DSA
  - and much more.
- Each chapter is a **CHEATSHEET**. It includes to-the-point explanation and relevant code snippets.
- Each concept can be covered quickly in at most 4 minutes.

With this, you will be able to crack any Coding Interview easily.

After reading this book, you will:

- Master C++ programming concepts. Have a strong mental model equivalent to programming at least 10K lines of C++ code.
- Strong implementation skills to optimize for performance.
- Clear interviews for full-time positions at high-tech companies.

This book is for:

- Students and developers preparing for Coding Interviews with C++ as their primary programming language.
- Experienced developers who wanted to revise their C++ concepts.

3

- Students who need a coding sheet to revise C++ topics quickly.

Get started with this book and change the equation of your career.

Book: **C++: Coding Cheatsheet: GOAT edition**

Authors (1): Wesley Kincaid

Published: March 2025 (Edition 1)

ISBN: 9798315652069

Pages: 33

Available on Amazon as e-Book and Paperback.

TABLE OF CONTENTS

C++ STL for ALGORITHMS & DATA STRUCTURES [DSA] 6

CLASS and OBJECTS: CHEATSHEET 10

INHERITANCE: CHEATSHEET 19

COMPOSITION: CHEATSHEET...26

SINGLETON PATTERN: CHEATSHEET...29

CONCLUDING NOTE 32

C++ STL for ALGORITHMS & DATA STRUCTURES [DSA]

Underlying data structure behind C++ STL data structures:

STL Container	Internal Data Structure
std::vector	**Dynamic array** (contiguous memory)
std::deque	**Double-ended queue** (array of fixed-size chunks)
std::list	**Doubly linked list**
std::forward_list	**Singly linked list**
std::stack	Adaptor (defaults to **std::deque**)
std::queue	Adaptor (defaults to **std::deque**)
std::priority_queue	Adaptor (defaults to **std::vector**, implemented as a heap)
std::set	**Red-Black Tree** (Self-balancing BST)
std::multiset	**Red-Black Tree** (Allows duplicates)
std::map	**Red-Black Tree** (Ordered key-value pairs)
std::multimap	**Red-Black Tree** (Allows duplicate keys)
std::unordered_set	**Hash Table** (unordered keys)
std::unordered_map	**Hash Table** (unordered key-value pairs)
std::unordered_multiset	**Hash Table** (Allows duplicate keys)
std::unordered_multimap	**Hash Table** (Allows duplicate key-value pairs)
std::bitset	**Fixed-size bit array**
std::array	**Fixed-size static array**

Use C++ STL for common data structures for solving coding problems:

Data Structure	C++ STL	Methods
Array	std::**array**<int, 10> arr;	size(), at(), front(), back(), fill(), swap()
Dynamic Array	std::**vector**<int> vec;	push_back(), pop_back(), insert(), erase(), size()

Linked List (LL)	std::**list**<int> lst;	push_back(), push_front(), pop_back(), pop_front(), insert(), erase(), size(), reverse()

Doubly Linked List (DLL)	std::**list**<int> lst;	auto it = dll.begin();
		it++;
		it--;

Stack	std::**stack**<int> st;	push(), pop(), top(), empty(), size()
Queue	std::**queue**<int> q;	push(), pop(), front(), back(), empty(), size()
Deque (Double-ended Queue)	std::**deque**<int> dq;	push_front(), push_back(), pop_front(), pop_back()
Hash Set	std::**unordered_set**<int> hashset;	insert(), erase(), find(), count(), bucket_count()
Hash Map	std::**unordered_map**<int, float> map;	insert(), find(), at/[], contains(), clear(), size()
Min Heap	std::**priority_queue**<int, vector<int>, greater<int>> pq;	std::**make_heap**(start, end), push(), pop(), top(), empty(), size()
Max Heap / Priority Queue	std::**priority_queue**<int> pq;	std::**make_heap**(start, end), push(), pop(), top(), empty(), size()
Adjacency List	**std::vector<std::vector<int>>** graph;	graph[u].push_back(v), graph[v].push_back(u)
Adjacency Matrix	std::vector<std::vector<int>> graph(**N, std::vector<int>(N, 0)**);	graph[u][v] = weight graph[u][v] = 1; (for unweighted graphs) graph.size(), clear()
Bitset (Fixed-size bit manipulation)	std::bitset<8> bs;	set(), reset(), flip(), test(), count(), size()

Ordered Set (uses BST/Red Black tree internally)	std::set<int> s;	insert(), erase(), find(), lower_bound(), upper_bound()
		
		for (int x : bstSet) {
		  cout << x << " ";
		}

Ordered Map	std::map<int, float> map;	insert(), find(), erase(), size(), clear()
Multiset (Sorted with Duplicates)	std::multiset<int> ms;	insert(), erase(), find(), count(), equal_range() [returns list of matching objects]
Multimap (Sorted Key-Value with Duplicates)	std::multimap<int, float> mmap;	insert(), find(), count(), equal_range()

Main methods you should be aware of for solving DSA coding problems:

Function	Purpose	Complexity
std::sort(vec.begin(), vec.end())	Sorts in ascending order (default) or custom order (cmp)	O(N log N)
std::partial_sort(vec.begin(), vec.begin() + 4, vec.end())	Partially sorts the first mid elements	O(N log K)
std::nth_element(vec.begin(), vec.begin() + N, vec.end())	Finds the **nth** smallest element (unsorted order)	O(N)
std::binary_search(vec.begin( ), vec.end(), value)	Checks if a value exists in a sorted array	O(log N)
std::lower_bound(vec.begin() , vec.end(), value)	Returns the first position where value can be inserted	O(log N)
std::upper_bound(vec.begin() , vec.end(), value)	Returns the first position where value is greater	O(log N)
std::make_heap(vec.begin(), vec.end())	Converts range into a heap	O(N)
std::stoi(str)	Converts string to int	O(1)
std::to_string(num)	Converts number to string	O(1)
str.std::substr(start_index, length)	Extracts substring	O(K)
std::find(str.begin(), str.end(), 'c')	Finds character	O(N)
std::next_permutation(s.begin(), s.end());	Generates next lexicographic permutation	O(N)
std::prev_permutation(s.begin(), s.end());	Generates previous lexicographic permutation	O(N)

std::gcd(a, b)	Computes GCD of a and b	O(log min(a, b))
std::lcm(a, b)	Computes LCM of a and b	O(log min(a, b))
std::min(a, b)	Returns the minimum of a and b	O(1)
std::max(a, b)	Returns the maximum of a and b	O(1)
std::min_element(arr.begin(), arr.end())	Returns an iterator to the minimum element in a range	O(N)
std::max_element(arr.begin(), arr.end())	Returns an iterator to the maximum element in a range	O(N)

CLASS and OBJECTS: CHEATSHEET

Foundation of OOP: this makes coding a DESIGN PROBLEM

OOP = Object Oriented Programming

- **Class definition and objects**

Class = member variables + member functions

Constructor = special function that gets called when an object is created to initialize data members.

Example of Node class:

```cpp
class Node {
public:
    // 2 Member variables
    int data;
    Node* next;
    // Constructor
    Node(int val) : data(val), next(nullptr) {}

    // Member function
    void display() {
        cout << "Node Data: " << data << endl;
    }
};
int main() {
    // Creating object of Node class
    Node node1(10);

    return 0;
}
```

- **Constructors and destructors**

Without constructor -> member variables have garbage value

Constructor Type	Purpose

Default Constructor	Initializes object with **default/ garbage values**. Provided by compiler or user-overridden.
Parameterized Constructor	Initializes object with **custom values**.
Copy Constructor	**Creates a copy** of an existing object. By default, does **shallow copy** (problem).
Move Constructor (C++11)	**Transfers ownership** of resources. Better than deep copy. Called when invoked using std::move(obj) **or** temporary object is assigned to another object **or** object is returned from a function
Explicit Constructor	**Prevents implicit conversions** from a single argument.

C++ code snippet with Node class:

Note: the code snippet demonstrates the concept of shallow and deep copy for copy constructor.

```cpp
class Node {
public:
    int data;
    Node* next;

    // Default Constructor (No parameters)
    Node() {
        data = 0; // Assign default values
        next = nullptr;
    }
    // Parameterized Constructor
    Node(int value) {
        data = value;
        next = nullptr;
    }
    // Copy Constructor
    Node(const Node& obj) {
        data = obj.data;
        // Shallow copy
        // Problem when obj is deleted (dangling pointer)
        // next = obj.next;
        // Deep copy of next
        if (obj.next) {
            // Recursively copy next nodes
            // Copy constructor called when object
```

```cpp
            // is passed by reference (*obj.next)
            next = new Node(*obj.next);
        } else {
            next = nullptr;
        }
        cout << "Copy Constructor Called\n";
    }
    // Move Constructor
    // Node&& R-value reference
    Node(Node&& obj) noexcept {
        data = obj.data;
        next = obj.next;
        obj.data = nullptr;
        obj.next = nullptr;
        cout << "Move Constructor Called\n";
    }
    // Explicit Constructor
    explicit Node(int value) { data = value; }
};

int main() {
    Node node1;  // Calls default constructor
    Node node2(10);  // Calls parameterized constructor
    Node node3 = node1;  // Calls copy constructor
    Node node4 = move(node1);  // Calls move constructor
    // Node node1 = 10; // Error: Implicit conversion prevented
    // Node node2(10); Explicit constructor if only data variable

    return 0;
}
```

Access Specifiers

Access Specifier	Scope
private	Only within the same class
protected	Within the same class & derived classes; Not outside in objects
public	Accessible anywhere

Polymorphism

- A function behaves differently.

- 2 types: Compile time and Runtime.

Compile-time polymorphism is achieved using:

- function overloading, operator overloading, or templates.

Function overloading:

C++ code snippet demonstrating an overloaded method add() which can add two integers or two floating point numbers:

```cpp
#include <iostream>
using namespace std;

// Function to add two integers
int add(int a, int b) {
    return a + b;
}

// Function to add two floating-point numbers
double add(double a, double b) {
    return a + b;
}

int main() {
    // Calls add(int, int)
    cout << "Sum of integers: " << add(2, 3) << endl;
    // Calls add(double, double)
    cout << "Sum of floats: " << add(2.5, 3.7) << endl;

    return 0;
}
```

Points:

- Two add functions have the **same name** but **different parameter types**.
- Correct function is **chosen at compile time** based on the **argument types**.

For compiler:

- Each overloaded function is given a **unique mangled name**.
- Compiler checks the function name, looks for a matching parameter list and **selects the most specific match**.
- If multiple overloads match equally well, the compiler **generates an error**.

Friend function and friend class

Friend function and class **can access private members** of the original class. Exception to encapsulation (hiding data) so use carefully. Note **friend property is not inherited**. Mainly used in **operator overloading** (like + for custom class).

C++ code snippet where private data of Node class can be accessed by LinkedList class and printData() method:

```cpp
class Node {
private:
    int data;

public:
    Node(int val) : data(val) {}

    // Declaring a friend function
    friend void printData(const Node& n);
    // Declaring LinkedList as a friend class
    friend class LinkedList;
};

// Friend function definition
void printData(const Node& n) {
    cout << "Friend Function: Node Data = " << n.data << endl;
}

class LinkedList {
public:
    void printNode(const Node& n) {
        cout << "Friend Class: Node Data = " << n.data << endl;
    }
};
```

Operator overloading

Operator overloading: Operators like +,-,*, << and others can be supported for custom class

C++ code snippet with Point class overloading addition (+) and << (for cout printing) operator:

```cpp
class Point {
private:
    int x, y;

public:
    Point(int a, int b) : x(a), y(b) {}

    Point operator+(const Point& p1, const Point& p2) {
        return Point(p1.x + p2.x, p1.y + p2.y);   // Accessing private
members
    }
    // Friend function for operator<< (Non-member function)
    friend ostream& operator<<(ostream& os, const Point& p);
};

// Friend function definition
ostream& operator<<(ostream& os, const Point& p) {
    os << "(" << p.x << ", " << p.y << ")";
    return os;
}

int main() {
    Point p1(2, 3), p2(4, 5);
    Point p3 = p1 + p2; // Calls the overloaded operator+
    cout << "Point: " << p3 << endl; // (6, 8)

    return 0;
}
```

Note:

- **operator+** can be a member function (as both operands are of same class).
- Cannot define **operator<<** as a member function as left operand (**std::cout**) is not a Point object.
- Must define **operator<<** as a **non-member function** and take **std::ostream&** as the first parameter.
- Use **friend** function to allow direct access to Point's private members.

Static member and static function

Static members and static functions are:

- associated with the class rather than instances (objects).

- share the same memory across all objects (one copy).
- can be accessed without creating an instance.
- declared using static keyword inside the class.
- must be defined outside the class to **allocate memory**.

C++ code snippet counting the number of objects created:

```cpp
#include <iostream>
using namespace std;

class Counter {
private:
    static int count;   // Static member variable (shared by all objects)

public:
    Counter() { count++; }   // Increment count on object creation
    static int getCount() { return count; } // Static function to access
count
};

// Definition of static variable (must be outside the class)
int Counter::count = 0;

int main() {
    Counter c1, c2, c3;
    cout << "Total objects created: " << Counter::getCount() << endl;
    return 0;
}
```

Feature	Static Member	Non-Static Member
Belongs To	Class (shared)	Object (unique per object)
Memory	Single copy for all objects	Separate copy per object
Access	ClassName::MemberName	object.MemberName
Function Access	Cannot access non-static members	Can access both static and non-static members
Use Case	Counters, shared configs	Per-object data

Constant member function

- const functions **do not modify object**.

16

- **cannot call non-const function** from a const function.
- Mark variable as mutable for exception where modification is needed.
- Non-const function can be overloaded as const function.

C++ code snippet of Stack class with const function top:

```cpp
class Stack {
private:
    vector<int> data;
    mutable int logCount;

public:
    void push(int val) { data.push_back(val); }
    void pop() { if (!data.empty()) data.pop_back(); }

    // Constant Member Function
    int top() const {
        ++logCount; // Exception: can be modified as it is mutable
        return data.back();
    }
};
```

Deleted function

- explicitly marked as deleted using **= delete;**.
- prevents the compiler from generating or using that function.

C++ code snippet of a Graph class which can have large adjacency lists, and deep copying is inefficient. We delete the copy constructor and copy assignment operator to prevent accidental copying.

```cpp
class Graph {
private:
    unordered_map<int, vector<int>> adjList;

public:
    Graph() = default;   // Default Constructor

    // Prevent copying (Deleted Functions)
    Graph(const Graph&) = delete;            // Delete Copy Constructor
    Graph& operator=(const Graph&) = delete; // Delete Copy Assignment
```

```
};
```

C++ code snippet of using deleted function to prevent implicit conversion of int to Stack where Stack has only one data member:

```
// Prevent implicit conversion of int to Stack
// Stack s2 = 5;
Stack(int) = delete;
```

INHERITANCE: CHEATSHEET

The most useful OOP feature.

Inheritance:

- **Base/parent class**:
- **Derived/child class**:

Example: Base class for **Shape**, Derived/child class for **Circle**

```cpp
#include <iostream>
#include <vector>

class Shape {
public:
    double area;
    void setArea(double a) { area = a; }
    void showArea() { std::cout << "Area: " << area << std::endl; }
};
class Circle : public Shape {
public:
    Circle(double radius) { setArea(3.14 * radius * radius); }
};

int main() {
    // Basic Inheritance
    Circle c(5);
    c.showArea();
}
```

Virtual Function

A **virtual function**: Expected to be overridden in child class (using override keyword). -> involve dynamic dispatch / resolved at runtime.

- Results in **runtime polymorphism** (function behave differently on runtime based on object).
- If function is not overridden, base class version is called.
  - o If it must be overridden, use **pure virtual function**.

```cpp
class Animal {
public:
    virtual void makeSound() { cout << "Some generic animal sound" <<
endl; }
};
class Dog : public Animal {
public:
    void makeSound() override { cout << "Woof!" << endl; }
};

int main() {
    // Virtual Functions & Polymorphism
    Animal* a1 = new Dog();
    a1->makeSound(); // Calls Dog's method
    delete a1;
}
```

Pure Virtual Function & Abstract Class

In C++, an abstract class is a class that has at least one **pure virtual function (function with = 0)**.

- enforce a common interface for all classes (like API)
- force function implementation, works with runtime polymorphism

We **cannot create an object for abstract class** because it is incomplete (at least one function has no definition) so it will result in **compile-time error**.

```cpp
class Graph {
protected:
    int numVertices;
public:
    Graph(int n) : numVertices(n) {}
    virtual void addEdge(int u, int v) = 0;
};
class AdjacencyListGraph : public Graph {
public:
    vector<vector<int>> adj;
    AdjacencyListGraph(int n) : Graph(n), adj(n) {}
    void addEdge(int u, int v) override {
        adj[u].push_back(v);
        adj[v].push_back(u);
```

```
        }
};

int main() {
    // Abstract Class - Graph
    AdjacencyListGraph g(5);
    g.addEdge(0, 1);
}
```

Diamond Problem & Virtual Inheritance

```
class Vehicle {
public:
    int speed;
    Vehicle() : speed(50) {}
};
class Car : virtual public Vehicle {};
class Truck : virtual public Vehicle {};
class Pickup : virtual public Car, virtual public Truck {};

int main() {
    // Diamond Problem Avoidance
    Pickup p;
    cout << "Pickup Speed: " << p.speed << endl;
}
```

Hiding

Overriding

- dynamic resolution
- base class member function is defined as "virtual"
- Same function name and signature.

Hiding

21

- static resolution
- base class member function is non-virtual.
- By default, derived class function is called. Derived class function can have different signature.
- To invoke, base class function use base_class::function_name

```cpp
class Base {
public:
    virtual void show() { cout << "Base show()" << endl; }
};

class Derived : public Base {
public:
    // Hides Base::show()
    void show(int x) { cout << "Derived show(" << x << ")" << endl; }
};

int main() {
    Derived d;
    d.show(10); // Calls Derived::show(int)
    // d.show(); // Compile-time error: Base::show() is hidden

    Base* b = &d;
    b->show(); // Calls Base::show() (because Derived::show() does
NOT override it)

    return 0;
}
```

To unhide the base class method, use "**using**":

```cpp
using Base::show; // Makes Base::show() visible in Derived

class Derived : public Base {
public:
    using Base::show; // Unhides Base::show()
    void show(int x) { cout << "Derived show(" << x << ")" << endl; }
};
```

Object slicing

- when an object of a derived class is assigned to a base class by value
- **loss of derived-class-specific data**
- Static resolution

To avoid this: **reference** of object of a derived class is assigned to a base class **pointer**.

```cpp
class Employee {
public:
    virtual void display() { cout << "Employee Details" << endl; }
};
class Manager : public Employee {
public:
    int teamSize = 5;
    void display() override { cout << "Manager Details, Team Size: "
<< teamSize << endl; }
};

int main() {
    Manager m;
    // Object Slicing: 'teamSize' is lost
    // Copy by value
    Employee e = m;
    // Calls Employee::display(), NOT Manager::display()
    e.display();

    Manager m;
    // Pointer to base class
    // but pointing to derived class object
    Employee* e = &m;
    // Calls Manager::display() dynamically
    e->display();
}
```

Final Keyword

If a particular member function of base class should not be modified by any derived class, declare the member function as "**final**".

- Prevent overriding.

- Results in **compile time error** if tried to override.
- Can only be used with virtual functions as non-virtual functions cannot be overridden.
- **Non-virtual** -> static resolution, **virtual** -> dynamic resolution.
- **Final** -> dynamic resolution.

```cpp
class Base {
public:
    virtual void show() final { cout << "Base show()" << endl; }
};
// class Derived : public Base {
// public:
//     void show() override {} // Error: show() is final in Base
// };
```

CRTP (Curiously Recurring Template Pattern)

```cpp
template <typename T>
class BaseCRTP {
public:
    void interface() { static_cast<T*>(this)->implementation(); }
};
class DerivedCRTP : public BaseCRTP<DerivedCRTP> {
public:
    void implementation() { cout << "Derived implementation" << endl; }
};

int main() {
    // CRTP
    DerivedCRTP d;
    d.interface();
}
```

Covariant Return Types

```cpp
class BaseReturn {
public:
    virtual BaseReturn* clone() { return new BaseReturn(*this); }
```

```
};
class DerivedReturn : public BaseReturn {
public:
    DerivedReturn* clone() override { return new DerivedReturn(*this); }
};

int main() {
    // Covariant Return Type
    BaseReturn* b = new DerivedReturn();
    BaseReturn* bClone = b->clone();
    delete b;
    delete bClone;
}
```

COMPOSITION: CHEATSHEET

Composition = has-a

Composition is when one class contains an object of another class as a member.

- Inheritance defines an "**is-a**" relationship (**Binary Search Tree BST** is a **Binary Tree BT**).
- Composition defines a "**has-a**" relationship (**BT** has a **Node**).

C++ code snippet of composition (BinaryTree class has a Node class):

```cpp
class Node {
public:
    int data;
    unique_ptr<Node> left, right;
    Node(int val) : data(val) {}
};

class BinaryTree {
private:
    unique_ptr<Node> root;
}
```

unique_ptr ensures Node is destroyed when BinaryTree is destroyed

Using Composition over inheritance:

- **Encapsulation**: Changes in the parent class do not affect other class.
- **Avoids Fragile Base Class Problem**: Inheritance forces subclass to depend on base class internals.
- **Multiple Behaviors**: Composition allows adding/removing behaviors at runtime. Need dynamic behavior changes (Robot changing AI modules).

Helps avoid **diamond problem** by breaking dependency chains:

```cpp
class Car : virtual public Vehicle {};
class Truck : virtual public Vehicle {};
```

 C++ CODING CHEATSHEET: GOAT edition ©

```
class Pickup : public Car, public Truck {};
```

In composition:

```
class Vehicle {
protected:
    int speed;
public:
    Vehicle() : speed(50) {}
};
class Pickup {
private:
    // Composition instead of inheritance
    Vehicle vehicle;
};
```

Objects in composition:

- Objects inside a class are destroyed when the class is destroyed.
- Use **unique_ptr** when object ownership should not be shared.
- Use **shared_ptr** when multiple classes share the same object.

Strategy Pattern allows objects to change behavior at runtime using composition.

PaymentProcessor can switch between CreditCardPayment and PayPalPayment dynamically.

```
class PaymentStrategy {
public:
    virtual void pay(int amount) = 0;
};
class CreditCardPayment : public PaymentStrategy {
public:
    void pay(int amount) override { cout << "Paid " << amount << " using
Credit Card\n"; }
};
class PayPalPayment : public PaymentStrategy {
public:
```

```cpp
        void pay(int amount) override { cout << "Paid " << amount << " using
PayPal\n"; }
};
class PaymentProcessor {
private:
    unique_ptr<PaymentStrategy> strategy;
public:
    void setStrategy(unique_ptr<PaymentStrategy> s) { strategy =
move(s); }
    void process(int amount) { strategy->pay(amount); }
};
```

Plugin system using composition dynamically adding and removing plugin:

```cpp
class PluginSystem {
private:
    vector<unique_ptr<Plugin>> plugins;
public:
    void addPlugin(unique_ptr<Plugin> plugin)
    {
        plugins.push_back(move(plugin));
    }
}
```

SINGLETON PATTERN: CHEATSHEET

Forcing so no one can duplicate your precious object

Singleton pattern:

- Only one object of a class exists and is shared by other objects.

C++ code snippet demonstrating Singleton pattern using:

- **shared_ptr**: better memory management using **reference counting**. Ensure destruction happen once and **avoid memory leak** (deleted only when not needed by any object)
- **call_once/once_flag** for **thread safety** (to avoid race condition while creating th first instance)

```cpp
#include <iostream>
#include <memory>    // For shared_ptr
#include <mutex>     // For thread safety

class Singleton {
public:
    // Function to get the singleton instance
    static std::shared_ptr<Singleton> getInstance() {
        std::call_once(initInstanceFlag, initSingleton);  // Ensures
only one instance is created
        return instance;
    }

    // Set a new value for the member variable
    void setData(int value) {
        data = value;
    }

    // Get the current value of the member variable
    int getData() const {
        return data;
    }

    // Manually destroy Singleton instance
    static void destroyInstance() {
```

```cpp
        instance.reset();   // Properly destroys the Singleton
    }
private:
    int data;   // Member variable that stores a value

    // Private constructor to prevent direct instantiation
    Singleton(int value = 0) : data(value) {
        std::cout << "Singleton Created with Value: " << data << "\n";
    }
    ~Singleton() {
        std::cout << "Singleton Destroyed\n";
    }
    // Deleted copy constructor and assignment operator
    Singleton(const Singleton&) = delete;
    Singleton& operator=(const Singleton&) = delete;

    // Static shared_ptr instance
    static std::shared_ptr<Singleton> instance;
    // Flag to ensure thread-safe initialization
    static std::once_flag initInstanceFlag;
    // Named function for initialization
    static void initSingleton() {
        instance.reset(new Singleton());
    }
};

// Define static members
std::shared_ptr<Singleton> Singleton::instance = nullptr;
std::once_flag Singleton::initInstanceFlag;

int main() {
    // Initialize Singleton with a specific value
    Singleton::init(42);

    // Get Singleton instance
    auto s1 = Singleton::getInstance();
    s1->showMessage();  // Output: Singleton Instance: Value = 42

    // Modify the Singleton's data
    s1->setData(100);
    std::cout << "Updated Value: " << s1->getData() << "\n";  // Output:
Updated Value: 100

    // Get another instance (same as s1)
    auto s2 = Singleton::getInstance();
    s2->showMessage();  // Output: Singleton Instance: Value = 100 (same
instance)
```

```cpp
    // Verify same instance
    if (s1 == s2) {
        std::cout << "Both instances are the same.\n";  // This will
print
    }

    // Manually destroy the Singleton instance
    Singleton::destroyInstance();

    return 0;
}
```

CONCLUDING NOTE

As a next step, you may randomly pick a concept from this book and dive deeper into it by researching on the topic and think how it is applicable for Data Structure and Algorithm problems or code design of a specific library.

If possible, work on it practically by writing code.

Go through open-source codebase and see if you can reason why a component for designed as it has been designed.

Remember, we are here to help you. If you have any doubts in a problem, you can contact us anytime.

C++ has proved to be one of the most influential programming languages for high performance. It will be the one of the few programming languages that will stay relevant even after 20 years.

We are at an inflection point as AI is redesigning the entire computing stack but C++ lives in the core of AI in the form of **DL frameworks and accelerator libraries which are all implemented in C++**.

Now on completing this book, you have conquered an essential programming skill.

Be a Deep Learning Engineer.